Empowerment Essentials that promote
Effective Advocacy for others

FROM THE
FRONT LINES

Great teachers advocate
for themselves first

DR. JOHN D. MCCONNELL

ISBN 978-1-959450-83-2 (softcover)
ISBN 978-1-959450-84-9 (ebook)

Printed in the United States of America.

Book Vine Press
2516 Highland Dr.
Palatine, IL 60067

ABOUT THE AUTHOR
DR. JOHN DAVID MCCONNELL

Growing up with five siblings, I learned the importance of sharing. We shared everything - food, clothes, shoes, money, cars, and information. The team captains (mom, dad, and oldest sister) have passed on, but the five of us who remain yet have each other. I've come to realize that because of my family community, I've never been alone. There are so many people trekking this life alone, without the feeling of connectivity. To this day, when my siblings choose to share information with me, I have no doubt it's from a sincere place of love and compassion. They want me to succeed! So, I'm "throwing my hat in the ring". Instead of packing up my classroom and vanishing silently into retirement, I've decided to pay it forward. As you turn the pages, I hope a kindred spirit connection occurs, and you adopt me as an honorary sibling.

Born and raised in Kansas City Kansas, John David McConnell received his Bachelor of Science degree at Saint Mary College in Leavenworth, Kansas. John has taught grades 2 through 8 over the past 27 years. 20 of those years have been with the Houston Independent School District. In 2016 John received his doctorate in sacred music from Christian Bible Institute & Seminary. John's war chest of badges includes Christian, father of two sons, educator, actor, singer, songwriter, Certified Christian Counselor, and author.

To Contact John McConnell:
Johndmac4@aol.com
832-865-0260

[ANTICIPATORY SET]

I have never served in the United States military, but I have gone to war. Although each state mandates the educational goals and objectives to be taught in school, it's the responsibility of administrators and teachers to bring the roadmap for the journey. Many students today receive accommodations or modifications for their instruction. Examples include preferential seating, shortened assignments, extended time, etc. Psychologists, Behavioral Specialists, and Diagnosticians have created labels to ensure that every child has learning conditions that are favorable for them. I support this framework of thought—that we should take measures to create the most nurturing learning environment for all children. It would; however, be irresponsible not to acknowledge just how great of a commander the teacher must be to effectively manage these young soldiers. The reason I'm using military jargon is to emphasize that life is (daily) blowing up children's lives in ways that make it virtually impossible to have the right response for every student in every moment. Their lives are shellshocked. They are fighting a war at home, in the streets, in the community—and teachers are tasked with loving them back to health, and arming them with strategies and weapons to fight. It is a war! School is the outlet for many kids to vent their frustrations. While kids view school as the place they feel safe, it's also the most polarizing place for so many. Course corrections are a daily necessity, but the reality is, the best accommodations we can establish for students is to develop strong meaningful relationships with them.

[PURPOSE]

So You Call Yourself A Teacher

Are you a motivator? What qualifies someone to wear that banner? Is it the formula they use in telling a story, or do we deem someone a successful motivator at the point in which we recognize their name or reputation? I've been inspired by so many people for different reasons. Not all of those encounters occurred within the framework of a traditional work relationship, or during extended periods where I was able to observe someone over several days. If you're paying attention, motivation happens in moments. I watched how they championed situations and gleaned from them. Actually, the true impact of the lessons I've learned, have been from the silent strength of those who simply purposed to win at life. As we journey from day to day, no one really expects to reach the end of themselves—their limit. Even when things happen outside of our expectation, we can usually develop a strategy to push forward. If we think long enough, there's always someone we can call who can work something out in our favor. In actuality that's called manipulation. Most people are very good at it, because it's a skill we develop from infancy. We are born self-centered, and growing out of it is something that must be learned. Cohabitating in this world and learning to trust and depend on one another is difficult. It may never be something you fully master, but life is so much more enjoyable when we realize we're not as much in control as we believe we are. Don't misunderstand me. Yes, we are the sum of the choices we make. But even when we choose a partner, a job, a path—we can't control the people or circumstances that are connected to those choices. If you ever live to experience the feeling of vulnerability, you'll find the terror that's heart-gripping. No doubt, this is not a place you'll ever plan to be. Take joy that this is a place that you can move from. That feeling of consistency that we've all known, may shift, but I hope to offer through this book a hopeful perspective that offers insight into a new level of motivation.

As someone who has lived more than 50 years, battled health challenges, experienced divorce, parenting, and other people's kids, I thought I'd step up to the podium. There's no rule for who gets to encourage you, but sometimes encouragement comes from people who share similar experiences. It's no secret that educating children in the classroom is important. Properly equipping teachers goes way beyond textbooks, pencils, and paper. If someone is to effectively advocate on behalf of children, they must be advocates of themselves first. Teachers Rise Up! Starting a new school year off right requires the right attitude. In order for you to be a difference maker, there must be something different about you—something that screams confidence and excitement. You must anticipate the 'give up attitude' that will try to surround you (oh yes it will). Keep in mind that all of that negativity won't come from students alone. A great deal of it will radiate from those in the fox holes with you—your coworkers.

A YEAR'S GROWTH...
FOR ME AS WELL AS MY STUDENTS

As an educator, it has always been the expectation that students demonstrate at least one year's growth from the beginning of the school year until the end. Some students show more, while others show less but yet there is always an expectation. No parent sends their child to school with empty hope. Even when parents know their child has extra deficits, they rely upon the magic of the school year to erase the fog and somehow present blossomed beings after nine months. This is nothing new, and as a matter of fact teachers will most of the time believe this magic of themselves. Without intentionally giving false hope, we encourage parents at the beginning of the school year that we're going to meet every need of their child as much as possible. The four words I'd like to focus on are: 'as much as possible'. What a powerful word—possibility. It's amazing that possibility for every person has an entirely different measure, and looks completely different for every living soul. As a 27 year classroom veteran, I don't profess to have all the answers. I don't hold the wisdom key that will unlock the door for your child's educational journey. However, I am absolutely certain that I have the answer for you—Educator. Never create a lesson plan for your students without creating one for yourself. I'm not talking about your script for the activities you wish to accomplish with the students. I'm making reference to the goals you will have accomplished personally by the end of the school year. The overarching philosophy I've always received as an educator, is that it has always been about the students. I'm challenging that framework in this book. I don't believe we minimize our effectiveness in anyway by making this bold statement:

IT'S ABOUT US. These three words have been the most pivotal for the first day of my instruction. I can no longer suggest to the young minds I wish to influence that my being there is all about them. Every teacher I work with is always happy to hear of a successful bond approval that includes a pay increase. If we're honest, teaching is providing a much more worthy paycheck than in years past.

In part, who I am determines the outcomes of those I influence. That's a message we send to children all the time. We tell them to be careful of the friends they choose, and to use wisdom when receiving advice from peers. But when they are enrolled in school, they're simply counted, sorted, and placed in the classroom of an adult that was screened and labeled as a "safe educator."

FOREWORD:
DR. BRIAN MCDONALD

I have had the pleasure of knowing John McConnell since 2005 when he was a Title IV Coordinator for the Houston Independent School District and I was a school principal. I was so impressed by his level of commitment to students that when the grant which funded his position ended, I recruited him to come to my school to teach middle school students. John embodied all that students need from a teacher. The majority of students at the school lived in poverty and in single-parent households. John was a true advocate and warrior for these kids.

At just over age 50, John has stepped up to the plate countless times, to bring peace to troubled situations. In this book, John shares his story to encourage others who are on the same winding road.

He believes in the importance of a quality education for children. He also believes that teachers need to be equipped beyond the basic necessities for managing a classroom. So much rides on the instructional core, defined by noted educational researcher Richard Elmore - as the relationship between the teacher, the content, and the student. What is vitally important is the relationship between teacher and student, especially students who deal with challenging situations in their daily lives. Teachers must therefore become fully empowered with what it truly means to advocate on one's behalf.

As a longtime teacher and now the superintendent of a large district, I couldn't agree more. One of my primary duties as a superintendent is to afford my instructional staff the best resources available. This book offers a hopeful perspective with insight into how important it is for the "carers" of the world to put energy and time into self-care. Parents always ask what more they can do to assist their child's teacher. Parents, after reading this book, many of those questions will be answered and your appreciation for teachers will quadruple.

As we're instructed every time we get on an airplane, we must remember to place the mask over our own mouth and nose before assisting others. I hope it resonates with every individual person who reads it, whether they are classroom teachers or in other professions.

PASADENA
Unified School District

BRIAN MCDONALD, ED.D. SUPERINTENDENT

Brian McDonald, Ed.D., has been Superintendent of the Pasadena Unified School District since 2014. He is an educational leader, adjunct professor, and a former principal and classroom teacher who is dedicated to providing an excellent educational experience for 15,000 PUSD students at 23 schools.

Under his leadership, PUSD has received major federal grants that created seven magnet schools, expanded dual language immersion programs to four languages (Armenian, French, Mandarin, and Spanish), developed a nationally-acclaimed math academy for accelerated learners, launched an innovative app development academy, and augmented college dual enrollment programs. Vibrant visual and performing arts and STEM programs are thriving with deep connections to the Pasadena area's rich cultural and scientific resources. With a strong focus on the social-emotional well-being of its students, PUSD is one of the only school districts with its own mental health department and was the first in the state to adopt a wellness policy.

Dr. McDonald led the development of a robust graduate profile, adopted in 2014, that created a shared vision for the cognitive, personal, and interpersonal competencies that students should have when they graduate. To graduate, 12th grade students must prepare and present a senior portfolio reflecting their learning, skills, and interests.

To balance the goals of optimizing the educational experience of its students with the budgetary constraints of statewide declining enrollment, Dr. McDonald led a reorganization, implemented a strategic budgeting process, and made painful but necessary budgetary reductions including the closure of four school campuses.

Early investments in 1:1 technology devices for students along with robust networks of instructional coaches and a teaching corps that recently completed a rewriting of the curriculum meant that PUSD was able to quickly shift to remote learning during the COVID pandemic. Vigorous emergency planning ensured that student meal service continued and that vaccines were administered as soon as they became available in January 2021.

Dr. McDonald collaborates extensively with parents, employees, and community partners to accelerate improvements and target resources to close achievement gaps between groups of students.

In November 2020, voters approved Measure O, the $516.3 million bond to increase student access to technology and upgrade classrooms and schools. In 2018, Pasadena voters approved a $21 million sales tax measure, resulting in the district receiving $7 million in additional revenue each year.

Dr. McDonald joined PUSD as Chief Academic Officer in October 2011. He has a Bachelor's degree from the University of Houston, a Master's from Texas Southern University, and a Doctorate in Educational Leadership from Sam Houston State University. He also serves as an adjunct professor at Azusa Pacific University. 12/2/20

CONTENTS

CHAPTER 1

CAST YOUR OWN LINE

Here goes a fishing analogy. To become an independent fisherman, you must learn to cast your line out into the water. In many cases, it's not about the distance, but the placement. If you are fishing from the shore, and your goal is to get your bait to the deepest part of the water, then it makes total sense for you to aim for the farthest distance. However sometimes there are large debris fields in the water, and depending upon the drift of your line, your bait and hook can be taken out. Where you cast your line determines the type of fish you will catch. Though schools of fish swim the deep water, many prefer to swim along the shoreline. Here is the connection. It's an enormous benefit to have cheerleaders in your corner, because so many people are without supporters to wave them toward the finish line. The only negative thing about having cheerleaders is when the cheerleader tries to become the coach. If you have goals and dreams for your life, it's difficult when other people try to forecast your journey. By some method, you must determine where you want to go, and how you'll get there. Our journey is littered with minefields, positioned to blow up our lives. Some situations would even have us question why we thought that particular dream was ever attainable. When the moment of clarity comes back, and yes it will come back, we must be able to recognize that the dream we are chasing is actually ours—not something put upon us. Strategies for doing anything are limitless. Choosing one is sometimes the hard task. The how doesn't nearly matter as much as the progress being made. The enemies of any vision are the excuses one uses to never begin the journey. Keep your reasons for your goals in front of you, because life will try to question them and talk you out of it. These three questions will help you to examine and redefine your purpose: What am I good at? What seems to bring me the most joy in my life? What is it that I would do everyday even without a paycheck?

John Steinbeck said, "I have come to believe that a great teacher is a great artist and that there are as few as there are any other great artists. Teaching might even be the greatest of the arts since the medium is the human mind and spirit."

Champion your moments. There are some things that no one can come close to you in succeeding at. Whatever you want to call it—innate ability, gift, talent; when it's all said and done, you are great at it. We don't always need someone else to talk us out of doing things. We're pretty good at robbing ourselves. After all, no one knows your list of failures better than you. I don't want to encourage you to forget that you've messed up before. I want you to feel empowered to use those lessons to capitalize on what went wrong and turn it into a massive success. The reality is everyone messes up—sometimes royally. How can we move our secret mistakes from the closet to the stage in a way that not only lifts us up, but motivates others? Tapping into that is a very large key toward advocating for others. When you can take a negative experience and begin to own it, you take the power away from what went wrong, which allows you to emphasize the fact that it did not destroy you. Most of us have heard the expression "whatever doesn't kill you makes you stronger" let's modify that, "whatever knocked you down isn't strong enough to keep you there." The word champion is defined by verb tense. Wearing the label of "Champion" requires Active winning (in the present tense). So what if it's taking you five years to see yourself as a winner. Some celebrations happen well after the fight, Just be sure to commemorate every victory.

I don't believe in coincidences. In my youth, I was more naïve and thought things happened by chance. I believe God has an awesome sense of humor. I think it really cracks him up when he has to create detours to get us to reroute our steps. I also think it baffles Him when he has to do it multiple times on the same road. It's not a coincidence, bad luck, or fate when you continue placing trust in a system that has proven to be unreliable for you. Not for all—but for YOU. If you were raised like me, I'm sure this exchange will sound familiar: "Mom, can I go to the party? Everybody's going to be there." Of course my mom's response was, "If everybody jumped off a cliff, would you do that too?" Experience may not be the BEST teacher, but it does teach us quite a bit. After we've watched others make mistakes, and live through some of our own, we begin to recognize those gentle nudges that make us pause and consider what we are about to say or do. Not everything should be a shock or surprise. Begin to follow your inner peace. If it feels wrong, most likely it probably is. If you're honest, I'm sure you can think of more than one occasion when you made an impulse purchase. You spent money that was assigned to something else on something far less important. It took weeks (maybe months) to dig yourself out of the hole you unnecessarily created. The only way to stop those debilitating cycles is to "wake up." Never go grocery shopping on an empty stomach—because you'll put things in your basket that you're craving, but are not on your grocery list. I know it seems silly, but some of the silliest sounding strategies will keep you out of trouble.

CHAPTER 2

Receive Each Day As A Gift

The most well laid plans are sometimes foiled by destruction. Often we see hopes of bright futures become distinguished by the atrocities of life. Accepting defeat is part of the life process, but to expect defeat is counterproductive. At different moments in our lives, things seemingly come out of nowhere and knock us off course. Sickness, disease, divorce, etc. No one should expect these things to happen, but we all should accept that something will. Acceptance and expectation rely on two different strengths. Acceptance says, "I acknowledge that this happened. This is how I feel about it." Expectation says, "I knew I had to prepare for this moment. I will rely on the strategies I've incorporated in my life to support me." Our thoughts and creativity are gifts. There is absolutely no one who imagines or creates exactly as you do. We can question why creative thoughts come when they do, but we'll never know the answer. We are all made different—set apart, not only by the way we look, but by nuances and expressions. Character studies are great. They give us insight into a person's perspective. I can adopt several of your habits, and even emulate them as 'best practices', but the more I try to morph into who you are, the more discouraged I will become.

No matter what occupation you're in, you should begin every day realizing that you have a tremendous amount of value. Because we're all uniquely made, no one has the imprint you possess. Your way of doing things is different than my way. How you approach situations, will be different than how I approach them. I believe we must approach each day without apologies, or second guessing ourselves. We must give ourselves permission to feel whatever it is we feel about what we're dealing with. It's OK to validate your emotions, just not be ruled by them. No one can beat you at being you, so throw out the filters and live truthfully.

Let's chop down some myths. When I first began teaching, I remember being told not to share too much about myself with the kids. "They don't need to know your business—just the lesson objectives ." I know that sounds like the safest way to proceed in a classroom setting, but kids with significant trust issues need more from you. Certain things you share about your life allow students to connect with you on a more personal level. They may start to see you as someone they can trust because they now see a side of you that makes you appear more human. Prepare yourself for the first time your students see you in the grocery store. It's so surreal. They hide behind their parents and begin whispering like you're an exhibit at the zoo. You can literally see their mind trying to correlate why you're there. Then they ask the question, "What are you doing here?"

Before Dr. Brian McDonald became the Superintendent of Schools in Pasadena, California, he was my building principal at Holland Middle School (Houston Independent School District). Every community has its own specific set of issues, and Dr. McDonald was sensitive to the needs of the Holland community. He challenged certain teachers to fill untraditional roles—to win back the trust we had somehow lost with the students. One summer a group of us attended a training called "Capturing Kids' Hearts ." The strategies we learned, practiced, and incorporated on our campus helped to facilitate a new culture of respect. We didn't hold our greetings until our students were in our classrooms, we met them with handshakes as they got off the buses, entered the building, as they walked through the hallways, as they entered the gym. Handshakes became required, because it was a sign of respect from teacher to student and from student to teacher. Teachers were required to individually greet students as they entered the classroom with a handshake and acknowledging them by name. Obviously, the handshake greeting was implemented prior to Covid-19. I'm simply making the point that good leadership turns over stones to uncover yet one more resource that can bring about a positive change. It should also be mentioned that the increase in our culture of respect translated into better teacher/student relationships, fewer tardies and absences, higher test scores, and a lower retention rate. If you successfully capture kids' hearts, without a doubt you have their attention.

One of the most traumatic things I ever experienced in my life was the killing of my mother. In 2006, I received a phone call and was told that my mother's neighbor's Pitbull got into her backyard as she was gardening and mauled her to death. No doubt, this is forever a part of my life experience. It plays a role in how I feel about dogs, and laws that protect those who own them. This is never a day one conversation in my classroom, but at some point throughout the school year, I share this with my students. No classroom is void of students who have experienced trauma. I definitely don't allow it to become a forum for comparing tragedies. It makes me relatable, and that's the best kind of teacher. Your story is a valuable part of you. How you choose to tell it is your gift to your students.

We're living in chaotic times-in the shadow of COVID-19, where doomsday prep is no longer viewed as extreme. There are literally hundreds of new occupations borne from the necessity of the times in which we live. If you've ever needed more encouragement to curb your procrastination, consider that many of the jobs in today's workforce will be irrelevant and obsolete five years from now. Here's a quote that's packed more muscle since the pandemic began: "Here today! Gone tomorrow!" The glass is no longer half empty. It's definitely half full. Stay clear of negativity which saps your energy and stunts your growth. I've learned that it's difficult to celebrate your assets when you haven't properly labeled your stuff. Usually labels are limiting, but not in this instance.

Ability to walk = Asset
Ability to talk = Asset
Ability to see = Asset
Ability to think = Asset

Take nothing for granted. Work harder to realize yourself worth. Find the most basic reason to celebrate each day because being here and having an opportunity to contribute is a GIFT!

"It's time to throw your hat in the ring."

CHAPTER 3

Expect Doors To Open

Your exact skills are needed for an exact situation, at an exact moment. Life is always challenging us, but when do we get to challenge life? I say we do it now. Don't wait any longer. Go as far as you can—using everything you have, and dare life to throw up a roadblock. If you don't exhaust the resources that are in your hand, you can't say you've given your all. Enter the contest. Write the song. Apply for the job. Don't allow the contrary voices in your head to rob you of what's yours. It used to confuse me to see contestants on American Idol who clearly were far from the standard the judges were seeking. To see the genuine heart break they displayed as the judges interrupted their auditions baffled me. Then I realized they had created a story in their mind. Either no one had ever told them they lacked singing ability, or they were successful in ignoring those who had. How great it must be to cancel out all inhibitions, and step onto a stage of competition. After all, you belong there until proven otherwise! Submit your proposal. Apply for the scholarship. Create a story in your mind that shows you images of you crossing the finish line 1st!

Everything that happens in your favor isn't just a coincidence. There are moments when everything lines up for you. Don't blow it off. It's significant because it's a sign you're on the right path.

Plastering classrooms with possibility is a requirement for every educator. What students hear, see, and experience in class every day must drip with slogans of hope and belief. No matter how despairing a students home life is, they must receive uplifting messages in school. Our voice does not become stronger than that of their parents, but it definitely competes. Think about that for a moment. Some primary school teachers have the same audience of students seven hours each school day. I doubt most parents have audience with their kids 35 hours per week (awake and engaged). But if they do, that's still only 50% of the time the teacher invests in them. If you've bought into that old cliché, "those who can't do, teach," perhaps you need to rethink this assignment you're accepting. To be effective in the classroom, you must first believe in yourself. The very fact that you graduated high school, earned a college degree, and attained a licensed certification in your state to be an educator demonstrates possibility. Draw from those experiences of accomplishment to cast vision of possibility for your students.

In most cases, when we begin to dream or idealize something big as a possibility, it won't be celebrated by all. I'll never understand why some people feel an obligation to verbally oppose what you're believing for. We sometimes call them haters, but they tend to view themselves as realists. Either way, to truly be in pursuit of something demands tunnel vision. When those moments of fatigue and frustration occur, there's no room for seeds of doubt if you're really going to win! I was a pretty good basketball player as a kid. I worked hard at it, and earned spots on my elementary, middle, and high school teams. I imagined I could make it to the NBA, but somewhere around the 10th grade my shortcomings on the basketball court began to overshadow my accomplishments. Once I began allowing my doubt to overpower my hope for making it to the NBA, my drive for it diminished drastically. When we offer students proven strategies for following their passion, we equip them to visualize what could one day become their reality.

I can't recall choosing this career. My recollection is that education chose me. In my early 20s I was working at an elementary school as a custodian for the Kansas City Missouri school district. I would notice students being singled out for disciplinary problems and ushered into the hallway for a chat with the teacher. On a few occasions, I asked if I could speak to the child. I always came up with something I thought was relatable to them—something that actually had nothing to do with school. Most of the time the conflict was about how the student responded to what another student had said or done. I challenged students to focus on things they were trying to earn, like spending the night at a friend's house on the weekend or getting a new video game because of a great week of conduct in school. Once I got kids to focus on incentives, reeling them in to do the task was simple. As those behaviors changed, teachers began to seek me in the hallways when they had trouble connecting with certain students. I enjoyed being part of the solution. More importantly, I was ecstatic about how my simple strategy could unlock so many more possibilities for students. I decided to enroll in a teaching program, began attending evening classes, and earned my teaching certification.

Just because you don't consider yourself "gifted", doesn't make it true. Your gift is the thing that allows you to do something in a way that is unique and that yields a prosperous outcome. Those outcomes may not manifest in a ridiculously large number of people, but perhaps only for a handful. Does the number of people helped by what you do determine whether or not what you have is special? I have a friend who asks me hard questions—not in an intrusive or offensive way, but very deliberate for the purpose of making me think. The way she frames things is without an apparent bias. Usually, I find myself sharing more than I ever intended. She has a way of allowing me to feel that my most honest response will yield me the greatest benefit. I'm sure there are others who experience that liberation when interacting with her, but until she recognizes the value of her unique ability, steps to nurture her talent will most likely not occur. She must be awakened to the FACT that what she has is truly a gift. Don't sleep on your special talents. Embrace them! Without embracing those unique things about ourselves, our special talents go unnurtured. Don't wait for a host of people to "sing your praises." Pay attention to your interactions with others and you will learn what sets you apart. Call it what it is. If not everyone can do it, then it's special—it's a "gift!"

For a moment, let's look at how two people with very similar talents utilize their opportunities for growth. Bobby learns that he is really good with his hands. His ability to make repairs is uncanny, and it's very rewarding for him to astonish homeowners by fixing things they considered "trash-worthy." Bobby's neighbor owns a company that makes magnetic business cards for vehicles. He convinced Bobby to monetize his talent by labeling himself as a handyman. He created two magnetic business cards for both sides of Bobby's truck that included Bobby's phone number and a slogan that says, "If I can't fix it, it's broken!" For the last Several years Bobby has made enough money from referrals in his community to comfortably make his house and truck payments—and he touts his neighbor as an excellent mentor.

In high school, Clark was nominated by one of his teachers to attend a youth leadership camp over the summer. The camp specialized in helping young people identify their interests and equipping them with an infrastructure to scale an idea into a lucrative business. At this camp, Clark learned that he had a talent for tinkering with and fixing things. He was referred to schools and programs that could enhance his skills and provide him a business structure for developing a sustainable business. Once Clark selected the college that best matched his interests, the school worked to find him a mentor who could assist Clark in creating a vision board. An awesome mentor connection happened for Clark, and the relationship equipped Clark with strategies for creating a home improvement business. His growth model was so efficient, that he was able to implement the same business plan in 23 different cities.

To be clear, there is no loser in either of the previous scenarios. Both Bobby and Clark experienced a level of success. Unfortunately Bobby didn't truly have a mentor. He had a neighbor who sold him an idea that fortunately helped meet a need he had. Clark on the other hand, had guidance and a safety net which provided a much clearer path for ultimate success. Life's reality is that most kids will only receive Bobby's level of opportunity. But the purpose of this book is to afford educators before thought to create more Clark opportunities for their students.

CHAPTER 4

APPLES AND ORANGES

Don't look for oranges when you've planted apple seeds. Your harvest will always reflect what you've sown. It's not magic. It's a proven science that no matter how you cultivate something, a duck is a duck-is a duck. Let's not confuse this with whether or not a person can change. People change all the time. I'm referring to the essence of a person. Even when motive causes us to behave a certain way, we remain essentially who we are. This may be hard to digest, but I believe we must retain core instincts in order to fulfill destiny. My purpose in this world may require me to have more aggressive tendencies than someone else. A florist, an archaeologist, and a book publisher are bound to have demonstrative traits that make them successful in their field. Many variables determine how people choose and swap careers throughout their lifetime, and I'm not suggesting labels or stereotypes for career placement. I am placing a focus on the fact that we have different demeanors for a reason. The healthiest thing a person can do is to reflect and examine their behavior daily. To never question how you respond to people and situations is very negligent. However, questioning your behavior doesn't automatically mean your actions were inappropriate. People will never give you permission to be who you truly are. It's a risk you must take, and for some the most difficult step of all.

From one year to the next, it's impossible to know what new devastating challenges await us. As a first year Second grade teacher in Kansas City Kansas, I remember the look on the faces of my students as we felt the rumble from the Oklahoma City bombing in 1995. I recall the bewilderment of my middle schoolers in Houston on 9/11 2001, as the news of the terrorist attacks in New York and Washington DC swept through our building like a brushfire. And 19 years later on that same Holland Middle school campus - I still shutter from the perplexed countenance of staff and students as we all tried to convince ourselves that the announcements of shutting down schools for a worldwide pandemic was a reality in 2020. And now, in 2022, as we push through to the other side of the pandemic, we have a resurgence of school shootings like the one in Uvalde, Texas – the second deadliest school shooting to occur in our nation.

Catastrophic events like these totally change people's idea of what feeling safe truly means. In the 90s, many were confused to learn that metal detectors were being added to the school landscape as protection from guns and knives. Who would've ever imagined that simply breathing the same air within a classroom would become a potential source of death? As a point of emphasis, children shifted from sharing pencils and pens, to stockpiling extra masks and sanitizer; to prevent sharing anything at all. Obviously, our methods for exchanging information with students is restructured every time a major world crisis occurs. Many parents have sought out options that will only allow their children to attend school virtually. The question isn't whether or not you embrace this philosophy of learning, but are you ready?

Are you prepared to bring kids into your world, even though they're still physically sitting in their own? Just as the world around us will continue to change, our teaching platforms must evolve as well. How will you excite the unexcitable child? Tricks, gimmicks, and emotional pleas won't work. Our 2020s kids have literally "seen it all ". You must earn their attention by showing them that you actually believe the words coming from your own mouth.

Although I exhausted a lot of words in a previous chapter explaining why 'coincidence' isn't really a thing, I do feel strongly that perception is reality. Even if it's not true that a student is failing a class, if he or she believes they are failing, then they are failing. The letter grade reflects that everything is fine, but the student may be experiencing regression in mastering the content. Really – I'm not trying to be deep or controversial, but I have had a love/hate relationship with letter grades my entire career as an educator. Grades are cumulative and show a snapshot of a window of time. But reality isn't a window of time. Reality is right now. No matter what grading system is being implemented where you teach, there are biases on both sides of the argument. To prevent debating one flamework of thought over the other, I'll simply fast-track to this statement. What your students demonstrate today is the most accurate measurement of their acuity. Let's take a look at this from totally outside of the classroom. It's possible to know all of the answers to the questions, without being able to apply any of the skills. What if I am attending a driver's education course, and I'm really struggling to feel confident when it comes to operating the vehicle? When I'm driving with my parents, I just can't seem to get it right. But somehow when my driving instructor is in the passenger seat, things seem to luckily happen in my favor. I'm not talking about coincidence. Remember, I got rid of that word. I'm talking about "the law of averages". The driving instructor is assigning a high rating, but the student feels very inadequate behind the steering wheel. One would say that the student needs to work on there confidence and self-esteem, and I would agree. But don't forget, perception is reality. How I perceive myself as a driver will be what manifests most of the time. I say we start focusing more on student mastery/outcomes, rather than keeping a punitive scorecard. I'm just saying…

CHAPTER 5

RISE ABOVE EVERY DIFFICULTY

It's important for us to use our energy to believe, rather than to fear. Human energy is very unique. It is a limited resource, yet renewable. Positive energy feeds off itself, causing our activity to feel beneficial and worthwhile. What this energy produces is what will sustain us until we can remanufacture it and repeat the cycle. The same is true with negativity. However, negative energy depletes what we have in store, and offers no motivation for growth. When we operate in a system of belief, we're moving and thriving. But when we are in fear, many things link themselves to us (doubt, regret, envy, strife).

How do you define success? It looks, fits, and feels different for everyone. If I have a pattern of anger that makes me respond to situations in ways I don't like, and I develop strategies that help me respond

more appropriately—that's success! Even my idea of "appropriate" is determined by how I view success for me. It involves truly getting to know yourself. It's easy to keep a list of what others do, but how about being retrospective? Be careful not to emulate others to the point of attempting to garner their success. What looks good on them might look horrible on you. Think of it as body type. All of our curves (though beautiful) are very different. How we accent our frame not only helps us feel good about our presentation, but assists others in seeing us looking good. No, success isn't about how other people think you look. My point is when you look better, you feel better—and when you feel better you perceive that others receive you better.

So let's delve deeper in this success talk. What makes someone consciously choose to become an educator? I've served on several teacher interview panels, and probably the most popular comment I hear from applicants is, "I love to empower children." Don't get me wrong. That's extremely important to know from every applicant. But it begs the question from me—"Have you been empowered?" This is the reason I feel this book should be required reading for all new teaching staff. Children don't need perfect people teaching them, but they do need people who are perfectly confident in what it means to be successful. Success isn't something you've arrived at. It's a journey. Not everyone has a strong sense of who they are as a person. Learning to use the deficits of life as combustible energy to thrive is a necessary practice for every human being. How much better would it be for all children if their teachers were secure in defining success for themselves before attempting to define it for them? If you're learning community does an offer these types of courses, be proactive and seek out trainings that offer strategies in self-actualization and personal goal strengthening.

CONNECT YOUR EFFORTS

In sports, commentators say it's important for athletes to have a short memory. When you've missed five consecutive jump shots, or thrown eight consecutive incomplete passes, it can get in your head to just stop shooting—just stop throwing the ball. It's also been said that once that first shot goes down, and that first reception occurs, the door becomes open. That works for franchise players. After all, they are paid the most money to keep shooting and throwing the ball. But the athlete who just signed a 10 day contract, and the reality for most of us is that we won't be afforded the luxury of so many failed attempts before being pulled to the bench. My suggestion is to have a long memory. It's impossible to build upon past accomplishments if you have forgotten their significance.

I teach kids every day that throughout their life they will often face rejection. And they must learn to use "no" as fuel to get to the place called "yes."

I've lived my life like many people; law abiding: working hard, going after it every day, being respectful to others. And at the end of the day, I'm tired because I've given myself. Going hard after dreams, acquiring some, but falling short of many. When you're good at a lot of things but without the opportunity to show it, it's frustrating.

When I was in the fourth grade, I won an award in my school district for writing the most impactful paper on the Industrial Revolution. I almost forgot about that. As a high school senior I had the second highest GPA and I spoke at graduation before my entire graduating class. I almost forgot about that. Several years ago at a Houston Independent School District board meeting, I was awarded a certificate of recognition for the impact of a song I had written about the Prejudice Awareness Summit that I helped facilitate for middle school students. I almost forgot about that. During my 20 years in that same district, I wrote and recorded 10 songs to be implemented in the programming of the safe and drug free schools department.

Now I realize it's important to remember what you've done. If we don't connect our efforts, then it's energy and time wasted. When we choose to remember, we draw lines from each occurrence and eventually we notice patterns of passion.

For so long I have been a writer of lyrics, a writer of songs, a playwright, an actor, an encourager, a teacher, a leader.

The words in this book are an embodiment of me. This is who I am.

I am motivated for school!

CHAPTER 6

TRUSTING COMMITMENTS

No matter how much we strategize and plan, some things will happen in life that are totally unaccounted for. Making commitments can be a very tricky thing, depending on your experiences. Some people feel they have received basically everything they've expected from their commitments, while others have been unfulfilled. Essentially a commitment is a binding agreement one makes to fulfill specific obligations. What's so unique about a commitment is that the obligation is one you place upon yourself. Obviously there are many forms of commitments—commitments to self, to others, as a spouse, parent, friend, etc. Not everyone has a heartbreak story, but some of us do. I never imagined my wife would walk away from me after 25 years of marriage, but it happened. The devastation felt insurmountable. At the time, there was so much blame I wanted to assign. But the reality was, life had to continue. My two young sons still needed follow-through in their lives.

Here are the facts. Every person is responsible for their level of commitment. Your involvement in someone's life can affect how difficult or easy it is for them to honor their pledges, but still the commitment is there's to fulfill. No matter who or what you're committed to, people have been taught to trust in commitment.

Vulnerability and paying it forward:

A promise I can definitely make to anyone pursuing goals, is that you will experience vulnerability. There is only one type of person that can live in entire life without experiencing a feeling of 'being in over your head'. Only someone with no ambition for growth will never be challenged with this necessary emotion. Like the need for sleep, food, and water, seasons of feeling inadequate or unavoidable. To be a better parent, friend, partner, teacher—a better anything—pushes us to find wisdom we don't currently possess. This is a difficult trade-off for many people because one must admit their dependence upon others. Even the most resilient people who have battled to regain composure to stand independently must allow others to help them. When we construct walls around ourselves regarding our own self sufficiency, it's hard to recognize when you're operating in pride. There should always be at least a few people in our lives with permission to tell us when we're feeling ourselves too much. By the way, no one ever wants to hear that they're thinking too highly of themselves. But when you're prideful it can repel people. So much distance is created, that no one is close enough to catch you before you fall. There is a line we must walk that is a balance between pride and contentment. Those who wrestle against The idea of embracing contentment must realize what contentment doesn't mean. It doesn't mean to be closed off to acquiring more.

The definition of contentment is: an inner sufficiency that keeps us at peace in spite of outward circumstances. A discontented person is never rich, but a contented person is always rich. If I am what I possess, and I lose those things—what am I? Learn to trust. Learn to thank. Learn to love. Learn to give.

It's important to know that someone is always watching. Different things draw people's attention, but just know that we are always under a microscope. Some years ago, I had a very unfortunate encounter as a third grade teacher. An accusation was made by a classroom aid, that I had inappropriately physically handled a student. To safeguard confidentiality, I will omit specific details. What I'd like to shine a light on is what did not occur. The person making the accusation, nor any campus administrator exchanged words or any form of communication with me. After school that evening, I received an email from my building principal to report directly to human resources the following morning and not to come to the school campus. Nothing felt relational about this exchange. The next day I was informed by an HR representative that my principal sent a detailed email regarding a reported incident, and I was thoroughly questioned about what had occurred. Additionally, I was told that a two-pronged investigation would ensue involving the police department and CPS (Child Protective Services). I was banned from my campus and instructed to discontinue all communication with any of my colleagues until the conclusion of the investigation. Nearly a month later, the investigation was concluded, and my suspension revoked. I had been cleared of any wrong doing, but the relationship between myself and the school administration had been tarnished. Although I was very confident that I had done nothing wrong, the people I worked with every day made a conscious decision to put my fate in the hands of people who didn't know me at all. It should be important to every principal that his or her staff believes they will fight to ensure they're treated fair. At the very least, I expected a personal call expressing that there had been an accusation that was totally out of line with my character—giving me a chance to respond to the allegation. This war is difficult enough on its own merits, but when you learn that you have a general who doesn't have your back, how are you supposed to feel? After you've been on the front lines for a while, you learn that things don't always happen the way they should. Sometimes people drop the ball, and you feel they've dropped you. These are situations that demand integrity. When you can push on despite being stepped on, you're growing.

Our challenges aren't only meant for us. They're also for the benefit of those who are watching. Just recently, a teacher who is aware of that situation I endured, called me and shared that she was currently in the middle of a very similar scenario. She called me to tell me that she watched how I championed my moment, not understanding how I had the strength to continue in spite of how I was treated. She said that if she had not watched me go through it, it would be difficult for her to believe she could successfully champion her trial. I was overjoyed to find out that things worked out in her favor. Not everyone is watching you with the intent to cause you harm. Some are actually drawing from your strength!

CHAPTER 7

YOUR LEGACY

President Joe Biden will long be remembered for saying, "We are battling for the soul of our nation." What do you want to be remembered for? Many times we think about this only after we're running on fumes, and about to give out. But this is a subject matter that one really should contemplate early in life. We don't want our legacy to be a byproduct of our life, but an intentional part. I know that once I've left this life, I'll be totally detached from all senses. Who attends my funeral, and how many people show up won't register at all with me (the person) because I will no longer exist. But I want to make such a deposit in this world, that when people hear of my passing it will cause them to have positive, impressionable memories of me.

Pledge to make a difference. Although we've all traveled different roads, here we are together at a very impressionable moment. The countdown has begun toward the start of a brand new school year. Positions are being filled, and you have one of them. Are you worthy? What will you do this school year that will forever change the lives of the students in your care? Will they be better or worse for having met you? In their adult life, will they remember you with a smile, or regret having ever crossed the threshold of your classroom? In the world of medicine, they have what's known as the Hippocratic Oath. Medical professionals vow to do no harm—to at least offer a better outcome for patient healthcare.

What assurances do we offer children and their families regarding their education?

My oldest son's first job was as a lifeguard. As he was fulfilling his training requirements, he learned some valuable information about human nature. The first law of human nature is self preservation. When a drowning victim is struggling to get above water for air, nothing is off-limits—including you (the lifeguard). When you need to breathe, the mind isn't multi-tasking. There's one singular goal—to get air by any means possible! Experienced lifeguards say it's easier to rescue an unconscious victim from the water, because there's no fight. Unknowingly conscious victims will impede their own rescue by violently flailing—rendering your aid impossible. No, our students shouldn't be viewed as victims, but many of them are flailing, failing, and drowning. How do you save someone who is actively fighting you? Is save even the best word? Some parents are convinced they don't need our help, and that attitude is also apparent in their children. As an educator, even when you're viewed as "a means to an end," you cannot take that personally. The relationships we establish with parents and students is different than our personal relationships. In a spousal relationship, it is extremely important to validate one another's significance. You don't have this luxury as an educator. You actually do yourself more harm expecting gratitude and gratefulness from parents and students. This is why you can't afford to show up empty. It's truly a battleground. Kids will say things to you that are totally out of bounds and not reflective of who you are. Expect it—you're in a war! In no way am I saying you should be disrespected, but if you lose focus, you lose the fight. The fact is parents and students need you more than they will ever admit, or even know. Sometimes years pass before students realize they're using life strategies you taught them. If it's more important that parents and students verbally give you credit for what you've deposited in them, I suggest you're more empty than you realize.

To remain—not just remain, but outlast hardships requires resolve. I once asked one of my mentors, a teacher who taught 40 years in the same school building, how did she remain in one place for so long? She responded, "I've always known that this is where I'm supposed to be. Once you figure that out, you must avoid excuses that try to convince you of anything else." *Resilience: The ability of a system to absorb shock, and recompile itself—sometimes in different ways.*

Having the fortitude to bounce back from adversity or misfortune.

Let's take some cues from nature when it comes to standing your ground. Redwood trees are a phenomenon of nature. I thought it hypocrisy to write about them without gazing up at them with my own eyes—so I planned a trip to the forests of California to view them for myself. I really must qualify how important this trip was for me. Three years ago I was diagnosed with diabetic retinopathy. Despite quality medical intervention, I continue to experience regression in my eyesight. Some menial tasks have become very difficult, but most important, my center of vision in both eyes is greatly compromised. I celebrate every morning I wake up with my sight. I spent hours beholding the enormity of it all. In comparison to these trees, I felt like a tiny speck on the forest floor. The embodiment I witnessed was other worldly.

I like how American author, John Steinbeck, described his encounter. "The Redwoods, once seen, leave a mark or create a vision that stays with you always… From them comes silence and awe. It's not only their unbelievable stature, nor the color which seems to shift and vary under your eyes, no, they are not like any trees we know, they are ambassadors from another time."

The tallest living thing on earth are massive coastal redwood trees, standing 300 feet. They can grow to have a diameter of 24 feet at their base and more than 360 feet tall (The height of a 35 story skyscraper). For comparison, the Statue of Liberty in New York stands 305 feet tall. Big Ben in London stands 315 feet tall. Remarkably for such massive trees, redwoods only have roots about 10 feet deep. They get their strength by extending their roots outward more than 50 feet, and twining them around the roots of other trees. Most live longer than 1000 years, and many of the largest ones are believed to be more than 2000 years old. Their bark can be up to 24 inches thick, and is resistant to many forest dangers such as fire, rot, and insects. I've heard it said that Redwoods are able to grow to be so high because they move and bend with the wind. The wisdom we are to extract from this is—If you stay rigid, eventually you'll break. This gives new meaning to the popular quote, "Life's not a sprint, it's a marathon."

CHAPTER 8

WHAT'S YOUR THING?

Inspiration is birthed from a place of comfort. For the majority of people, creativity is accessed more readily when you feel really good about the moment you're in. The season you're experiencing might not be comfortable, but the moment (the space you're in, what's surrounding you, the environment) creates peace, which allows you to create. There is a saying, "if mama's happy, everyone's happy." What it means is, whoever is responsible for dictating the flow of the home (schedules, meals, chores, etc.) will do so from a reservoir of their emotions. They will lead happily-willingly-lovingly, or gloomy –grudgingly-spitefully. If we're honest, not feeling our best minimizes our output. This doesn't mean your functionality can't be great. I understand that our human nature can tap into a strength that overcomes what seems possible. Many are familiar with what's now known as Michael Jordan's "flu game" in 1997 during game 5 of the NBA finals—when he willed his body to score 38 points for the victory against the Utah Jazz. I'm sure you have your own personal testimonials of times you pulled out a win while physically living a personal trauma. Those are rare feats and attest to just how powerful the human condition truly is. Years ago I learned that if there's unrest surrounding me, it's very difficult for me to be expressive with my gifts. Just as important as learning what stresses us out, is coming into the knowledge of what sets us free. I absolutely love going to the movies. Now I enjoy watching Netflix movies at home with the family, but there's something enormously special about watching movies on the big screen at a theater. It's hard to explain, but that atmosphere lifts me literally. I think my blood pressure is probably at the perfect number when I'm experiencing a theater movie, because that's just how relaxed it makes me. I have a list I won't share of other things I enjoy that put me in that "special place", but my point is-we all need to be able to let go at times so we can become reacquainted or introduced to the feeling of pure inspiration.

Trust

Trusting can be a very difficult thing to do, especially if your experiences have left you on the bad end of things. Here I'm discussing you releasing or planting your trust in a process, not you being a trustworthy person. On many occasions I have honestly felt that my relationship with "trust" has been very one-sided. For some reason I'm usually in the posture of having to justify why I deserve certain benefits, rather than being immediately celebrated. It's not always apparent that I am the first choice in the selection process. Someone had to turn down the offer before it was awarded to me. And I usually must provide supplementary data and a research paper as a rationale for a salary adjustment. When you're never the favored candidate, never recruited, and always forced to audition, it's inevitable that skepticism grows. This isn't headed where you think. I'm not going to cheer you on to be the underdog grudgingly proving you belong at the front of the pack. Acknowledge the emotion, but don't become a victim. Yes it hurts to always have to prove your worth, but everyone's path is different. Learn to embrace your path and trust that what you've invested will afford you the greatest opportunity.

To effectively offer our students the most we possibly can as their teacher, requires us to learn more about who we are as individuals. When we have keen awareness for how we process and take in new information, it empowers us to be more responsive to how our students can thrive when they receive information based on their learning style. Teachable moments are lost when we are unable to recognize whether or not our students are making transformative connections to the lessons we teach.

There are many books and classes available for assisting teachers with resources for the subject matter their teaching, but how do you know when you're actually making and building lasting connections with your students? What do you base it on? If you're someone who struggles emotionally with being "present" consistently, especially when dealing with a personal crisis—how do you know you've captured your students during the moments they're in front of you? After all, we get really good at masking what's really going on. If we can easily hide from our students, what makes us think they can't hide from us? We must confront our behaviors, because that will give us insight to ourselves—inevitably assisting us in noticing what's going on in our classrooms.

The way to finish what you've started is to remain excited about it. Let's talk about getting that joy. For this illustration, imagine joy as "the light ", and sadness as "the dark." It's been hypothesized that light is pure. It is not equal to darkness, as a light drives out darkness. When you enter a dark room and turn on the light, there's nowhere for darkness to hide—it simply vanishes. So let's agree that to see things clearly (from the right perspective), we must adequately fill it with light. In the dark, we labor to find the right outfit. With light, the outfit is quickly revealed. In an unlit parking lot, it's a chore to find your vehicle at night. In the light of day, we can identify it—even from a far distance. Still using the illustration that light is equivalent to joy, what causes us to move away from what we once considered "our joy?" I'm notorious for really great ideas. Years ago, I actually began praying that God would drop inquisitive thoughts in my head for ad campaigns and business ventures. Can't blame God on this one. The ideas came. I like a quote from Joseph Campbell that says, "The cave you fear to enter, holds the treasure you seek." It's not enough to know the requirements. Something intrinsically must capture our heart to keep us trained on the mission. Good ideas manifest quickly, but God ideas must be cultivated. I'm still talking about joy and light. There was something you were tremendously excited about that had your undivided attention. What happened? Somehow you allowed what once was illuminated to be stacked in a dark corner. Shine the light on it again. Reclaim your excitement for it!

We've all met people who are ridiculously talented to do certain things. It's like they were born to do it, and requires very little effort on their part. Sometimes people fall into roles because they are naturally dynamic. Is that a good thing? Of course it makes total sense, and could be viewed as negligent not to strongly encourage someone to pursue a job that poses no obvious down-side. But will that job be enough to stimulate the mind, evoke passion, or challenge their creativity? Every year in the world of sports, we hear stories about young athletes who make choices that 100% contradict the path they're on. Some choices we can attribute to being young and naïve. But sometimes people implode from the pressure of being in the wrong place. When you're making millions of dollars but your soul is unfulfilled, you're viewed as a crazy person to walk away from it. Without the proper counsel/support, we add things to our lives that complicate and mask the real issue. To quote John Steinbeck, "A sad soul can kill quicker than a germ."

CHAPTER 9

Who's Cosigning For You?

Who you choose to allow in your inter-sanctum is extremely important. The people connected to you affect you—and are affected by you. When others are added to your process/filter, how they think and feel about the issues you discuss become part of any deliberations you engage in. After the fact how many times have we said, "I should've followed my first mind?" When others validate half-processed decisions, we get stuck right there. We hear our cheerleaders rooting, and that gives us confidence to suspend deliberations. Adding people to your "process" gives them an unspoken consent to offer their opinion.

It feels amazing when people choose us, but sometimes it's better when we choose them first. A good mentor goes beyond being available when you reach out to them for help. Someone who is truly "for you" will see the turns in the road way before you get there and make sure your hands are firmly on the controls. I challenge you to choose mentors who want to play a significant role in your life. Georgia Berry, my fourth grade teacher in 1977, was also my first building principal in 1995. Mrs. Berry was not only my fourth grade teacher, but the mother of one of my good friends, Tyrone. Most mornings she and Tyrone would arrive on campus super early (as good teachers do). Rather than go inside the school, Tyrone walked a mile to my house, had breakfast with my family, and walked to school with me. This was the routine from first grade through sixth grade. There were many Fridays where instead of me walking home

after school, I got in their car to go home with them for the weekend. Tyrone had many breakfasts at my house, and I had several dinners at his. When I made it to the fourth grade, and found out Mrs. Berry was my teacher, it felt like Christmas! In a sense, she was like my second mom, so I can only imagine how difficult that must've been for her to balance the roles. District policy didn't allow her to have her own son as a student, yet there I was instead of Tyrone. I tested the boundaries of that relationship from time to time, but she was very consistent in keeping me in line. I am intentionally providing this extensive background to emphasize the importance of Mrs. Berry as a mentor. Because of a healthy, nurturing relationship with Mrs. Barry, seeds were planted for the relationships I formed with teachers going forward. From one school year to the next, these bonds helped assign value to my self-esteem. These were not just teachers, but developmental assets in my life. In 1994, a very close member of my home and church family—Pearl Copeland agreed to mentor me as a student-teacher. And over the summer, the first and only principal I interviewed with for my very first teaching position, was Georgia Berry. All those years she planted, watered, and protected me as an investment. And when I was in full bloom, she picked me as a member of her team. Choose mentors who also choose you.

Everything is connected. Stop acting as though it's not. From the moment you wake up each day, until the second you close your eyes to sleep—everything you say, do, and think matters. You probably think I'm saying that it matters to other people. No—I'm saying it matters to you. Perhaps not at that very moment, but in retrospect.

I remember a training I had to attend in Keller, Texas. Keller is near Dallas—about a 4 1/2 hour drive from my house in Houston. The training ended at 1 PM. It had been raining pretty hard all morning, but I was determined to get back to Houston before dark. It was really pouring, and I recall thinking, "Everybody's driving way too fast." Up ahead I noticed a tow truck sitting still in the middle of the highway. It seemed we all noticed at the same time, because there was a sea of simultaneous brake lights. It would be a miracle to survive this moment without crashing the first brand new car I've ever purchased for myself.

As my heart was beating through my chest, an older model El Camino in the lane to my right locked brakes and slid into a concrete barrier on the side of the highway. I noticed the driver and his expression of helplessness as he was smashing into that wall. I was so thankful to have come through it all unscathed, but I felt so bad for that driver. He was all I could think about the entire drive home. Is he injured? Where was he headed? How many inconveniences must he overcome as a result of those six seconds? I prayed for that man several times as I realized how blessed and fortunate I was to be free to continue...—Unburdened by the loss. Thank you God for your grace! I knew immediately how much it mattered that I was shielded from that accident. On two previous occasions I played the role of accident victim. I suffered loss and it will forever be part of my experience. But thankfully roles change—and when they do, it's important to employ empathy. Sometimes being able to relate to misfortune can cause you to be an integral part of someone else's journey towards recovery.

CHAPTER 10

Purpose To Finish Strong From The Beginning

Glance at your problem while gazing at your solution. In other words, don't try to act like your problems don't exist. Give them the credibility they deserve, but not power and prestige in your life. Train your focus on what it will take to solve your problems. Ask the right questions. How can I overcome this hurdle? How many adjustments do I need to make in my budget to allow for this debt to be paid? Unacknowledged problems never begin to feel insecure and decide to leave your life. It's always there, and usually amassing more girth the longer it's avoided. Most people shell problems until they FEEL they have a better capacity to deal with them. At this very moment, there is a very tiny plumbing leak in my laundry room ceiling—originating from the bathroom above it. Last month I cut a hole in the sheet rock to allow the drips to fall into a bucket. I wouldn't call that a permanent solution by any stretch of the imagination. But I just have not felt like dealing with that issue yet. As long as the toilet above that ceiling continues to get flushed, the leak Shell continue. It will never vanish without a resolve. At some point, I'll have to abandon my excuses regarding my feelings, the amount of money it will require, the extra energy involved, etc.

To quote Bishop T.D. Jakes, "Feelings aren't facts. They fluctuate. Feelings are wonderful things to have until they have you." In order for educators to be instrumental in teaching young people to be problem solvers, we must first teach them to be good managers. Outstanding managers thrive by changing the optics. I don't mean they act as though what's happening isn't really happening. They simply become efficient in having the correct response. It's not a problem if you see it as something that simply requires a specific reaction. We may not find agreement here regarding problem/solution, action/reaction. But I think we can agree that something must be done to bring change.

In most K-12 educational settings, vocabulary words have been integral for many years. Vocabulary plays a fundamental role in the reading process. It's foundational, and necessary for a reader's comprehension. We used to limit the vocabulary focus to the subject of reading, but over the last several years our understanding has revealed that a focus on vocabulary benefit students in all subject areas. When words are highlighted and emphasized before the introduction of the lesson content, students are made aware early that these are the words that essentially will unlock their understanding of the information they are about to learn. Whether students are reading, listening to an oral presentation, or viewing a slideshow, they cannot fully understand the information without knowing what most of the words mean. Students learn the meanings of most words indirectly, through everyday experiences with oral and written language. However, gatekeepers/educators must be vigilant and regularly check for understanding.

Throughout these pages I've been spot lighting many key vocabulary words for success in education. Ready for another one? Let's talk about compassion. When you don't have compassion for something, no announcement is necessary. It's written all over your face, and reflected in your body language. There's a look that screams, "I really want to be here right now!" But we all know the look that says, "If these kids ask me one more question, I'm going to lose my mind!" Kids are very perceptive. It's not always about what you say, but how you say it. Even your expression during independent work time can communicate to your students that you'd rather be somewhere else. I loved—loved—loved my sixth-grade teacher, Jacqueline Sobering. I remember her wanting to spend so much time with us that she gave us incentives to earn Saturday morning fun time at her apartment complex. Based on classroom achievements, groupings of students were selected to hang out with the teacher some Saturday mornings. I'm talking about an indelible memory I have from 42 years ago. Her excitement/compassion for wanting to spend time with her students made me want to do good work for her. The other sixth grade classes were jealous because their teachers weren't about to surrender their unpaid time to students. I've never been a dog person, but Ms. Sobering had a black Labrador Retriever we played with on those Saturdays. I recall being very uncomfortable around the dog, but more excited to spend time with my teacher on the weekend. Do you realize how powerful that is? As educators, we have the power to move kids beyond their comfort level/fears by demonstrating compassion! As a disclaimer, nothing was done inappropriately. The teacher had the proper consents to host these gatherings, and some parents would always volunteer to assist. I'm not trying to rally for you to give your weekends to your students. More than likely, it's against your district's policy. I'm simply pointing out that if you sow genuine compassion into your work with kids, they will remember you forever!

Allow me to qualify what makes me credible for this message. No one joining a fitness center and seeking a personal trainer scans the kiosk for the most out of shape looking person. Please don't misunderstand me. I'm not suggesting anything in the arena of judgment, but we all are guilty of it—judgment. We choose people to speak into our lives based on what qualifies them to do so. After all, people who are inexperienced in any field must attend the school of 'hard knocks' and learn the pitfalls before they can ride high tides of success. I'm choosing the fitness trainer with the sculpted physique. Surely this person has amassed strategies based on discipline, and can be instrumental in casting vision for my fitness journey—right? I don't want you to choose my voice—my words—my strategies. My hope is that you're able to see that you and I are not that different. The universities I attended, and my professional affiliations are meaningless to you if there's no correlation in our experiences. Where you end up in life is the most important thing. Most people say the journey is more important. I disagree. Even if I can appreciate the setbacks I've experienced, and I'm able to journal—being intentionally reflective daily, that's not enough. Where I'm from and the totality of all my experiences and life strategies must propel me to arrive. Arrive where? Where you want to be—where you need to be—where you deserve to be!

Most nights I go to sleep listening to sermons preached by Adrian Rogers. There are several things I'd like to point out here. Adrian Rogers left this life 17 years ago in 2005. The majority of the lessons I watch on YouTube were from a pulpit in Memphis, Tennessee (a place I've never lived). Pastor Rogers was white, and I am not. One might question how the words of someone who is no longer alive, and not where I'm from can have so much influence in my being inspired. My best advice for your encouragement is: When you realize what you're hearing feels like nourishment, refuel there as often as possible—despite the packaging. You've chosen a very worthy, yet challenging profession. Be fully present in each moment to ensure you're making the largest impact possible for yourself and your students. Purpose now (Day 1) that your finish will be just as intentional as your start.

"THE MASSIVE REDWOODS"
[FROM CHAPTER 7]

CPSIA information can be obtained
at www.ICGtesting.com
Printed in the USA
JSHW051432030223
37228JS00004B/11

9 781959 450832